Be An Expert!™

High Fliers

Erin Kelly

Children's Press®
An imprint of Scholastic Inc.

Contents

Know the Names

Be an expert! Get to know the names of these high fliers.

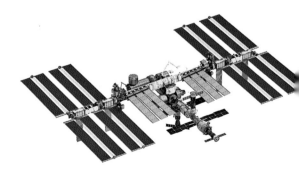

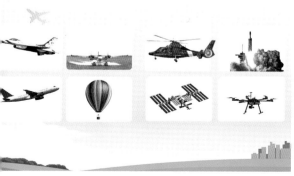

Airplanes

Here they come.
Time to take off!

airplane

Flying High

Q: How many people can fit on an airplane?

A: The biggest airplane can fit more than 500 **passengers**!

Helicopters

Up they go.

Whoosh, whoosh, whoosh!

Zoom In

Find these parts on the helicopters.

blade

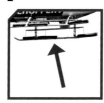
landing skids

main rotor

tail rotor

Seaplanes
They can land on water.

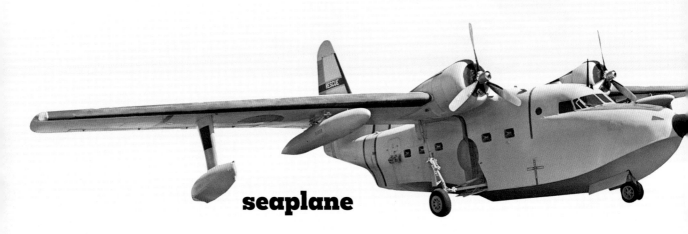

seaplane

Military Jets

They can fly upside down.

Falcons

Lightning

Flying High

Q: Is it hard to fly a military jet?

A: Yes. **Pilots** like me learn not to vomit when the plane twists and turns.

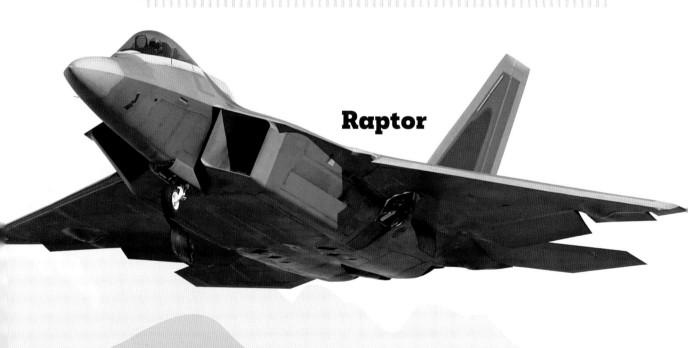

Raptor

Hot-Air Balloons

Up, up, and away!

Zoom In

Find these parts in the big picture.

basket

burners

skirt

envelope

Drones

They fly without a pilot.

camera drone

<u>remote control</u>

delivery drone

Expert Fact

Some drones take photos from the sky. Some deliver pizzas!

PIZZA
PIZZA

Rockets

They go into space.

Three, two, one, blast off!

Zoom In

Find these parts in the big picture.

booster

exhaust

launch tower

nose cone

Space Station

It goes around Earth.

Expert Fact

Astronauts live and work on the International Space Station. They learn about space!

International Space Station

All the High Fliers

Coming in for a landing.
Good work, high fliers!

1.

2.

5.

6.

Expert Quiz

Do you know the names of these high fliers? Then you are an expert! See if someone else can name them too!

3.

4.

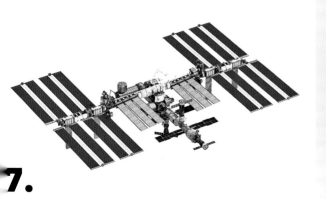

7.

8.

Answers: 1. Military jet. 2. Seaplane. 3. Helicopter. 4. Rocket. 5. Airplane. 6. Hot-air balloon. 7. Space station. 8. Drone.

Expert Gear

An **astronaut** wears a spacesuit.

It has **lights**. ➡

It has a **backpack**.

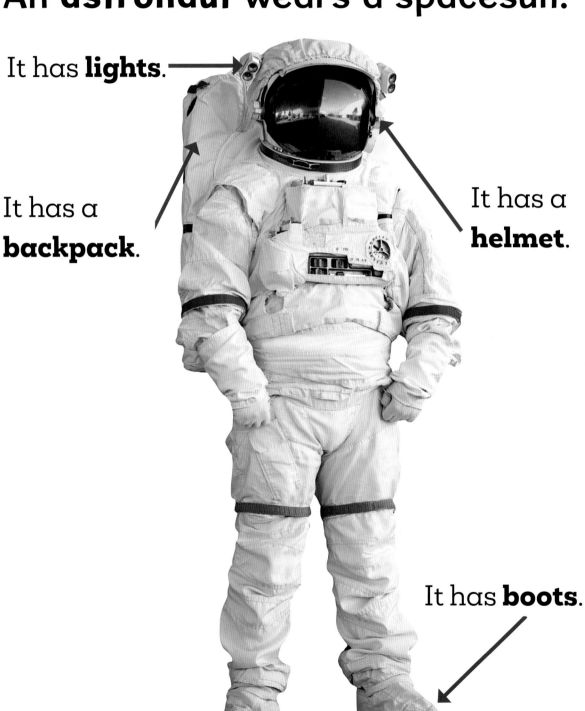

It has a **helmet**.

It has **boots**.

Glossary

astronaut (AS-truh-nawt): a person who goes to space.

passenger (PAS-un-jer): a person who is traveling on a boat or train, or in a car or an airplane.

pilot (PYE-luht): the person who flies an aircraft. This pilot flies a plane!

remote control (ri-MOTE CON-trole): what you use to control something from far away.

Index

Library of Congress Cataloging-in-Publication Data

Names: Kelly, Erin Suzanne, 1965- author.

Title: High fliers/Erin Kelly.

Description: New York: Children's Press, an imprint of Scholastic Inc., 2020. | Series: Be an expert! | "Produced by Spooky Cheetah Press." | Includes ind

Audience: Grades K-1 (provided by Children's Press)

Identifiers: LCCN 2019027855| ISBN 9780531127629 (library binding) | ISBN 9780531132432 (paperback)

Subjects: LCSH: Airplanes—Juvenile literature. | Helicopters—Juvenile literature. | Aeronautics—Juvenile literature. | Airplanes, Military—Juvenile literat

Classification: LCC TL547 .K942 2020 | DDC 629.13—dc23

LC record available at https://clicktime.symantec.com/3AncdRubc5GWGmvpdtY1f517Vc?u=https%3A%2F%2Flccn.loc.gov%2F2019027855

Printed in Heshan, China 62

SCHOLASTIC, CHILDREN'S PRESS, BE AN EXPERT!™, and associated logos are trademarks and/or registered trademarks of Scholastic Inc.

1 2 3 4 5 6 7 8 9 10 R 29 28 27 26 25 24 23 22 21 20

Scholastic Inc., 557 Broadway, New York, NY 10012.

Art direction and design by THREE DOGS DESIGN LLC.

Photos ©: cover: IgorBukhlin/iStockphoto; cover boy and throughout: McIninch/iStockphoto; back cover helicopter and throughout: DigtialStorm/iStoc photo; spine and throughout: sethstock/Shutterstock; 1 main: guvendemir/iStockphoto; 1 sign: BaLL LunLa/Shutterstock; 2 top left and throughout: kick iStockphoto; 2 top right and throughout: Darren Brode/Dreamstime; 2 center right and throughout: Vladone/iStockphoto; 2 bottom left: Luis Louro/Shu stock; 2 bottom right and throughout: 3DSculptor/iStockphoto; 3 top left and throughout: icemanphotos/Shutterstock; 3 top right: CT757fan/iStockpho 3 center left: Olly Curtis/Future Publishing/Shutterstock; 3 center right and throughout: Jonathan William Mitchell/age fotostock; 3 bottom right: MediaF duction/iStockphoto; 4-5 background: VectorPot/Shutterstock; 4-5 jet: EnginKorkmaz/iStockphoto; 5 girl: Rawpixel.com/Shutterstock; 5 pilot: michaelj iStockphoto; 6-7 background: Liana Monica Bordei/iStockphoto; 7 chopper: Tom Dowd/Dreamstime; 7 girl and throughout: Gelpi/Shutterstock; 7 hat ar throughout: Floortje/iStockphoto; 8-9 background: MerggyR/iStockphoto; 8 seaplane: breckeni/iStockphoto; 9 boy and throughout: McIninch/iStockph 10-11 background: MerggyR/iStockphoto; 10 falcons: Charles F McCarthy/Shutterstock; 10 lightning: DigtialStorm/iStockphoto; 11 raptor: CT757fan/iStoc photo; 11 boy: Rawpixel/iStockphoto; 11 pilot: kupicoo/iStockphoto; 12-13 background: MerggyR/iStockphoto; 13 balloons and throughout: sankai/iStockp 14-15 delivery drone: sarawuth702/iStockphoto; 14-15 grass and throughout: Nataniil/iStockphoto; 14 camera drone: Valentin Wolf/imageBROKER/Shutte stock; 14 boy: pookpiik/iStockphoto; 16-17: SpaceX/Polaris/Newscom; 17 night sky: SLdesign/Shutterstock; 18-19: 3DSculptor/iStockphoto; 19 girl: YinYa iStockphoto; 21 child: Luis Louro/Shutterstock; 21 drone: Vlad_Alex/iStockphoto; 22: Pgiam/iStockphoto; 23 space: NikoNomad/Shutterstock; 23 girl: FamVeld/iStockphoto; 23 pilot: michaeljung/iStockphoto; 23 remote: pookpiik/iStockphoto.